SUCCESS

NATOYA CHAMPION

Mercy B Publications

hi@MercyBCarruthers.com

Ordering Information:
Quantity sales. Special discounts are available on quantity purchases by corporations, associations, and others. For details, contact the publisher at the e-mail address above.

Printed in the United States of America

For Shekinah, Zachary, Alexia and Christian; the heart plays a vital role in supplying the oxygen and nutrients to the body through the blood. The heart also happens to have four chambers. You four are my heart; I am because of you.

-Mama

INTRODUCTION

Suc·cess

/səkˈses/

noun

the accomplishment of an aim or purpose.

What exactly is success to you?

The definition of success up above is a generic definition that I pulled from Google. However, before we dive into this chapter and this book, I want to be very clear that neither Google nor am I, myself, able to truly define success.

In my opinion, there is no universal definition of the word that will be suitable for everyone. The reason for this is that I believe the word success is very subjective. It's a word that means something different to everyone that you encounter, being that everyone's goals differ. While some people may look at success in terms of professional success, there are some who may look at success in terms of their life, their happiness, family and/or good health.

Simply put, what I view as success may be different from what you view as success. There is not one specific way to be successful. Success is a mindset that must be adapted in order to accomplish your goals. It is the state or condition of meeting a defined range of goals and expectations that you (or someone else) set for yourself. As long as you are happy with your outcome, that is all that matters.

There is no specific recipe for success. You can't add a bunch of things to a pot, cook it, and it come out the same way every time. However, the steps and habits that a successful person take and develop in order to achieve success are pretty universal.

Regardless of what your end goal may be, to be successful at achieving any goal that you give yourself, you must first know what success is to you. What will your life look like once you have reached the success that you desire? Now that you know that… how do you plan on achieving it? Are you aware that you must be consistent and remain positive—replacing negative thoughts with positive ones that will motivate you to keep you going? You should remain passionate and hard working so that you can achieve that goal and ultimately embrace that success. You must also be creative and focused on your goal at all times, constantly learning and looking to grow, going over and above to stay up to date.

In my opinion, there are about thirteen steps, give or take, that I feel need to be completed and followed in order to reach full success. Those steps include planning, spending time alone, experiencing failure, staying well rested, being self accountable, staying unbiased and listening. Staying away from comfortability (complacency), having a good mentor and patience, staying true to your purpose, not seeking validation, staying authentic and engaged are all a part of those steps.

Those steps that I listed don't necessarily have to be done in that order, but you should make yourself familiar with them all. Every last one of them completes the puzzle of success, and if one piece gets overlooked or misplaced then your puzzle will be incomplete. Therefore, to assist you in becoming familiar with them, I will be breaking down those steps and how they relate to success throughout this book. I'll also be giving examples that I have witnessed and/or experienced myself on each of those steps and how they hindered or helped someone that I know to become successful.

I hope that you find your way to success with this guidebook and that you share it with someone else who is currently on their path to success but may need a little guidance to help them along the way.

1

PLAN

Plan

/plan/

NOUN

A DETAILED PROPOSAL for doing or achieving something.

Do you have a goal that you would like to achieve or that you are trying to attain? Well, may I ask… what's stopping you from accomplishing it? Could it be your lack of planning?

. . .

'A goal without a plan is just a wish'. What does this quote mean to you? To me, it means that without breaking my goals down into miniature actionable steps that I can work towards on how to achieve my goal, then ultimately, I'm just daydreaming. Long story short, if I ever want to live life the way that I dream it, I have to provide the foundation necessary to achieve it, and then put the work in.

When I was younger, I didn't quite understand this quote, but I can blatantly recall hearing it all of the time while I was growing up. However, as time went on, my understanding of the quote grew, and I realize just how true this quote is. Planning is your own personal map to success. It provides you with every turn, highway, tunnel, and exit that you can expect to come across as you are on your journey, prior to your arrival.

What's the first question you ask when someone tells you what their goals and aspirations are? If you're anything like me, it would be *'what steps have you taken so far to achieve them, or what steps do you plan on taking to achieve them?'* If their response to that was, that they have no plan, they were simply trusting that what is for them will be for them, you would look at them like they were crazy. I know I would. How can anyone expect their dream to come to fruition without a plan and hard work?

The thing is, though... that is exactly what a lot of people are guilty of. They believe that they can manifest something without them having to actually put in any of their time or themselves into their craft. They don't take the time to set intentions, invest in any of the required work, or give the time necessary in order to have what they are claiming for themselves.

From my own experience, I've found that the reason a lot of people fail is because they don't plan. A lot of people just go with the flow of things. Allowing life to happen to them as it pleases. Unfortunately, it's why many people, in my opinion, do not succeed at their goals. Being aware of this fact taught me early on that in order to be successful, I needed to plan.

A plan is how you intend to take action to achieve your goal. It is the spine of your goal. Without it, your goal could never be achieved. Planning provides us with the direction on how to accomplish our goals while giving us the opportunity to precisely define the objectives and steps needed to achieve them. It allows us to manage our time and maximize our productivity so that we aren't doing twice the work or wasting our time and/or our resources due to the lack of planning. Planning also helps us to critically assess the goal to see if it is realistic.

For that reason, I have two planners—one for work and one for my home life, that I use faithfully in order to assist me with my time management, growth, and development. As a wife, mother of four, and a full-time retail leader, my plate runs over, a lot. It's the reason that I plan as extensively as I do because it's the only way that I can keep a balance to my life and any kind of organization to my world.

By organizing your days, weeks, and months into a planner or a calendar, it allows you to see the bigger picture of your schedule and to always know what to expect. Another benefit I've found with keeping a planner is that you are able to track your progress. When you document your tasks, goals, activities, and plans and then complete them and cross them out, you are able to look back and see what was accomplished. You can also learn a lot about your processes and yourself from a planner. Are you a procrastinator or do you tackle your tasks ASAP?

. . .

PLANNERS ALSO HELP you to remember the important things as well as the not so important stuff. This can in turn assist you in improving your memory. I've noticed that when I write things down, I'm more inclined to remember them.

LASTLY, planners help you to organize your day and your life. Sometimes, when we are making plans for our days, there is no flow. For instance, I knew someone who worked for Children Services a while back. When they had home visits, they would sit down with their planner and MapQuest their clients' addresses so that they could determine which of their clients lived closest to each other.

THEIR DAY WOULD START with the home visit of a client that was the furthest from their home and gradually make its way back in the direction of their home, hitting all of the clients that were in route. They did this to ensure that their day and travels were not scattered.

SOMETIMES, things make sense and sometimes it doesn't. You may scatter things throughout the day without realizing it and having it in plain view allows you to move it around so that your days can flow easier.

BESIDES MY PLANNERS, I also use my Outlook calendar. It's helpful for me because depending on how busy my day is, I may overlook something in my planner, but having the instant notification on my phone or laptop allows me to stay on top of appointments and tasks. Outlook also aids me in saving time by tracking recurring meetings or events so that I don't have to manually schedule individual events every time they occur.

MY WORK PLANNER has exactly what you would think it has in it… tasks related to my work life. Meetings, deadlines, pay days, holidays and days off as well as passwords and logins to my work-related accounts. As for my home planner, you'll find stuff like important dates related to my children and husband, vacations, recitals, plays, meal planning, and more.

I'VE EVEN STARTED my children with maintaining a planner. Let's say, for instance that they sign up to bring something to a party at school—they are then required to put it in the planner on the correlating day and time. Not only does it save me from finding out the morning of that I have to provide something for them for school, but it also teaches them the responsibility of keeping a planner. As they grow, they will continue to understand the importance of planning and organizing.

As for my Outlook calendar, you may find a blend of both planners in my outlook calendar. Among other things, it's the last resort in case I've overlooked something. When I put things in that calendar, I make it a point to have it alert me five to thirty minutes before the event (depending on whether I need to travel or not) just in case I didn't remember.

I maintain order to my life and my planners by scratching things out that I may have done or that I've had to move around to another day or time. I find myself making adjustments often. There was a time when I would get upset because I didn't meet the deadline that I gave to myself, but now, I've learned to go with the flow.

The thing about planning though is that you have to be committed, remain consistent and be intentional. Be committed and consistent about intentionally doing the work needed to achieve your goal. Plan intentionally and completely by giving yourself deadlines, stay focused on what you want and not what you don't want. Don't dwell on things that you cannot control. However, the things that you *can* control, plan around them.

Now, here is another thing about planning… sometimes, even when you plan, it may not go as you plan—that's life. Sometimes, you'll have to show how flexible you are by adjusting your plans. You'll find that the allotted time that you've given yourself doesn't work anymore or something more important needs to be pushed up and that's fine. There is nothing wrong with adjusting the plan as long as you stick to the goal.

How many years have you given yourself a New Year's resolution that didn't make it past week two? Yep, I was guilty of that too. I found that the reason my resolutions didn't make it through the year with me was because I didn't plan or in some cases, I didn't adjust my plan to make it doable. Had I planned or adjusted the plan on how I would achieve my resolution, I would have been able to ensure that I got the end result that I wanted.

. . .

The same goes for that paper or book that you need to write. If you outline (plan what you are going to write about) in advance, it will help your words to flow easier. Many people claim writer's block because they didn't plan their words. Instead, they waited until the last minute and decided to wing it and their lack of planning shows through the work that they submit.

The thing about planning is that it allows us to pace ourselves. Instead of cramming a lot of work in at one time, which can be overwhelming and lead to procrastination, planning allows you to knock out smaller goals a little at a time. It makes achieving your goal a lot more feasible and attainable.

If you are a procrastinator, like many people can be when the goals that they set for themselves seem overwhelming, planning can also provide you with the needed motivation to get started and to complete the task. Anytime that I have planned effectively and stuck to it, seeing the small progress that I've made always motivated me to continue with my plan. Sometimes, it even motivates me to do more to see my goal get achieved even quicker.

. . .

Even deeper than planning, is writing down your goals. I believe it was Erykah Badu who said, *'write it down on real paper with a real pencil and watch how real it gets.'* From experience, I can attest to this. When you write down your goals, you are more likely to achieve them. Something about seeing them makes them real and gives you clarity on what direction you need to go in. It also provides you with the motivation to get it done.

I was listening to Steve Harvey's speech, Steps To Success, and he said something to the extent of *'if you are speeding unknowingly, because a truck is blocking the sign that tells you the speed limit and you get pulled over, you'll still get a ticket. Regardless of whether you seen the sign or not, it is written into law already.'* This applies to writing your goal down as well. Even if you don't look at the written goal every day, something about writing it down embeds it into your mind. It makes it law within you, guaranteeing that you will make it happen.

2

ALONE

A·lone
/əˈlōn/

adjective

1. having no one else present.

Let me start by saying that I think people get alone and lonely confused for each other. They are not the same. Being alone is physical… simply put, you are not with anyone else. Loneliness is emotional… mental. It's a feeling that describes your mental state. See? Two very different things.

. . .

Need another example? Okay, the pandemic. Some people felt alone because they were home alone, literally and some people were lonely even while being in the house with some of their family members.

One thing that this pandemic has shown me, and many others, is that being alone creates the atmosphere for success. For many new entrepreneurs, they used the alone time during this pandemic to grow personally and to bring to life their goals and dreams or revamp them to make them work for the times.

When the pandemic first began, I, like many people, sat at home for a few weeks, twiddling my thumbs, praying that this would all go away so life could go back to normal. However, after a few weeks turned into a few months, I figured out that normal wouldn't be normal ever again. That prompted me to make changes and adjustments (look at that… I had to adjust my original plan) in order to maintain, and excel, at that.

The alone time that the pandemic presented allowed me to tap into myself and figure out what I needed/wanted to do for my betterment and the betterment of my family. It also allowed me the opportunity to boost my self confidence and self esteem. Things that I doubted myself on before were no longer a question. The alone time gave me the opportunity to become more comfortable with myself, my skills, my weaknesses and my strengths.

THE PANDEMIC PROVED among many other things that there is beauty in being alone, though for some people, it may be hard to see. Some of the beauty is that you can hear your *own* voice. Sometimes, our thoughts and actions get meddled by those of the people around us, without our knowledge. We take on the morals, beliefs and thought processes of our friends and family and claim them as our own.

NOT JUST THAT, but we also lose focus being distracted by the family and friends around us. There are many people who feel that they had to leave their hometown and go where they could be alone, in order to be successful. They knew that had they stayed, they would not have had the discipline to stay on the path to success with the influences of family and friends around them.

. . .

ANOTHER BEAUTIFUL FACTOR of being alone is that you don't have outsiders' expectations weighing you down. For a lot of people, the expectations of family members and friends hinders their ability to do what they believe is best for them. Instead of trusting that they are capable of making the best decision for their life, they allow others to dictate how their life should play out.

WANT to know something else being alone does for you? It aids you in evaluating the relationships that you have with the people in your life and the relationships that you want with any newcomers. Being alone makes you deliberate about the relationships you allow in your life.

WE CAN'T FORGET that the people we surround ourselves with have the power to make or break us just as much as we have the power to make or break ourselves. When I was a child/teenager, I could not fathom this. I didn't understand what it means to be picky and selective about the people who I allowed into my circle. As I grew into womanhood, I realized that the quote *'birds of a feather flock together'* was the truth. Normally, the people you pick as friends are typically the people that you have the most in common with.

. . .

EVEN DEEPER THAN THAT, I realized that a lot of my "friends" could not come where I was going. Not because I didn't want them to, but because they didn't want to. My idea of success was just not for them and that was ultimately fine. Especially when I considered the influence, they had over me even without me realizing it.

NOW, that's not to say that the road to success can't be lonely because many times, you'll find that it is. Just as well, being lonely may intertwine with being alone on a few occasions as well. However, loneliness is an emotion that will pass, eventually.

AS YOU CONTINUE to grow and develop, your circle may change. Again, that's perfectly fine. Anything that doesn't change and evolve is in a sense dead… even the wildlife grows and changes. The journey is your time to grow and focus while learning new things about life and yourself in the process. For that reason, you may need to cut out the additional noise and chatter from the outside world.

HAVE you ever been in a situation (relationship) that no longer served you and the moment that you let it go everything starts happening for you? Exactly. When you hold onto things that no longer serve you, you delay your growth. There is nothing wrong with being alone… especially when the company you are with no longer serves you.

CUTTING out the outside noise will help you find clarity. You'll be able to focus on the things that matter the most to you. Things that you may not have had the ability to pay attention to due to the distractions.

AS I BEGAN to elevate in my career, I simply could not do some of the same things that I used to have a ball doing. Taking it a step further, I could not do them with the same people I used to love doing them with. Our energies didn't mesh any longer. Their idea of success did not match mine. They didn't understand the sacrifices that I was making or the time and energy that I was investing. Not that there was anything wrong with them or me, it's just that we no longer had the same interests. It was a tough pill to swallow for a while, until I realized that I had to release them in order to elevate.

I KNOW someone who was in a relationship with someone for a few years off and on. While they were together, she was stagnant and didn't even realize it. She had always been a bright young lady, but her choice of company shaded her vision on what she wanted from her life. She had always wanted to be successful. She had plans and talent but the relationship that she was in didn't feed her what she needed. There was no praise or encouragement. Instead, many times, her ex would discourage her. In my opinion, it was because he knew that she had the potential to be great. I think he was afraid of her leaving him after she reached her highest level, but that is just speculation.

ANYWAY, the only time this young lady could focus on herself and her growth was when they were not on good terms and broken up. For instance, they broke up one time and she immediately went and got her associates degree. Then, they got back together and once again, she was stagnant. She couldn't find a job and she couldn't see herself exceling past the place that she was in. Her vision began and ended with the guy and the relationship she was in.

WHEN SHE FINALLY DID FIND A JOB, IT was a job that someone told her about, and it was a minimum wage job that she was overqualified for. She would go to the job everyday feeling like she didn't belong, but she didn't have the drive to look for anything more because she was complacent with her life and being with her then significant other. When they broke up though, baby! She got a call back from a job that she had forgotten that she'd even applied for while she was with her ex. This job made her happier, paid more, gave her better hours, and even paid for her to go back to school. With that, she enrolled back in school for her bachelor's degree. She was in school for eighteen hours every week and working forty plus hours at her job every week.

THE MOMENT that she detached herself from her ex and his energy, she started exceling and things started to look up for her. That right there is the power of being alone.

3

FAILURE

F ail·ure

/ˈfālyər/

NOUN

LACK OF SUCCESS.

THOMAS EDISON ONCE SAID, *'I have not failed. I've just found ten thousand ways that will not work.'* Is this how you view failure? Are you determined to not allow failure to win by not giving up? If so, you are on the right path!

. . .

GOOGLE DEFINES failure as a lack of success but what exactly constitutes as a failure to you? I ask because lack of success can still be success, right? What about when you have failed forward and still wound up in a place beyond where you started? Is failure when the outcome of your goal or desire does not meet your expectations? Or what about if your success does not come about in accordance to your plan? In that case, is your failure a failure or a success?

WHEN YOU 'FAIL' at something, do you continue to try to different ways to become successful at that task or do you give up? Are you resilient? Do you take your failures and adjust what is needed in order to see success on your next go around? Is it possible that failures only occur when and where you stop trying to achieve a goal?

CARDI B WAS onto something when she said, *"knock me down nine times but I get up ten"*. Many people have this notion that failure is not a part of success. That couldn't be furthest from the truth. Failure is one of the founding blocks of success, it's also the one thing most people are afraid of. It's why most people never go after their dreams… unfortunately, it's also why a lot of people stop trying to accomplish their goals.

. . .

To not experience any failures in life while attempting to achieve a goal means that you have already perfected whatever you are trying to succeed at. Failure, without realizing it, gives you the opportunity to learn and grow. It exposes the areas that you may have difficulties getting to in order to have your expected outcomes.

Failure, if you ask me, is about perception… kind of like success. If you perceive that your failure is a bad thing, then that is what it will be. If you perceive it to be a learning experience… something to show you that you have room for improvement, then again, that is what it will be.

For instance, most businesses don't start seeing profits until after five years and many don't succeed past the first five years. Do you think that it is because they aren't seeing the profits that they wish to see in the first five years and so they give up? What could have been the outcome if they had stuck it out a little bit longer? This is why failure doesn't mean quit. It means to find more ways to be successful. What can be done to change this failure into a success?

. . .

For some reason, we have been conditioned to believe that if we fail, it's bad. It starts in adolescence. As children in school, we're taught that if we get failing grades, then we weren't paying attention or that we are slacking off. That isn't necessarily true though.

You can pay attention all day to something and still fail at it when it's time to complete the task. Ask the many people who struggle with math despite having tutors and paying attention in the class.

The conditioning that failure is bad carries on with people throughout their lives and then taken even further. It gets perpetuated that if they fail at something, that means that they should give up because they aren't good at it. I'm not people. I believe that if I fail at something, clearly, I'm not doing something right and I need to adjust (there goes that word again) my actions in order to get the outcome that I want.

Failure teaches us to learn from previous mistakes therefore, you won't make that mistake a second or third time. Hence why there is a such thing as a second chance.

. . .

To me, failure is like the prerequisite to success. It teaches you about consistency, creativity, motivation and dedication. Actually, you learn more through failure than you do from success. What does success really teach you anyway? The moment most people succeed at something, they are no longer trying to learn new ways to succeed.

Failure also has the ability to build your confidence. Through failure, we become ourselves. Our losses and failures build our character. We also learn how to develop the necessary skills in order to succeed at not just our task but in life as well. After each failed attempt, we come back to the table a little bit smarter; with more knowledge on how to better achieve our goals.

Also, keep in mind that failure can be successful in itself. There are plenty of people who had plans and goals outlined, and they failed at it, but they succeeded at something else. People find success in their "accidents" all of the time.

Just think about all of the children who wouldn't know how to walk. In order for them to reach success, they first have to fail. When infants are learning to walk, they fall many times. They bump into things, fall, and more. However, they don't stop. Instead, they remain persistent. They continuously get back up and try again until they accomplish the goal of walking. Once they have walking down, they go on to learn to run, skip, jump and more.

THE SAME GOES for children learning to ride a bike or to skate. No matter how many bruised and scratched elbows and knees they get, they continue with their goal of learning to ride skates and/or a bike.

WANT to know how you can change the perception of your failures and use them for success?

FIRST, **celebrate when you fail the same way you do when you succeed.** Acknowledge the effort that you put in and the work you've done, despite it not working out the way that you anticipated it to. Realize that you are one step closer to success. Remember, we put the negative connotation on failure. Let's change it by starting with ourselves.

. . .

Don't allow the fear of failing keep you from playing the game. If you don't join the game, there's only one option available. At least if you are in the game, you have the options to learn and possibly win also.

Always prepare for the worse but plan for the best. You should never walk into a situation without weighing on the possibility that you may feel just like you may succeed.

So ultimately, failure is everything but fun. It can be embarrassing, frustrating and ground-breaking. However, it's also an opportunity to reflect, learn and regroup. Just because we fail doesn't mean that we should stop trying. Remember, fall down seven times and stand up eight.

4

REST

Chapter 4- Rest

rest

/rest/

verb

TO CEASE work or movement in order to relax, refresh oneself, or recover strength.

. . .

There is this episode of The Cosby Show that I love, and it coincides with this chapter perfectly. In season 5, episode seventeen Rudy has a movie party with some of her friends. The movie that Cliff chooses for her and her friends to watch is a movie that they don't want to see. Kenny brings a movie with him that Rudy is not allowed to watch and after Cliff has put the movie that he rented for them on and left the children to their party, they change the movie. When Claire comes home from work, she catches them watching the movie they told Rudy that she was not allowed to watch and after everyone leaves, she gets reprimanded for it.

In response to this, she composes a list of complaints that she gives to Cliff and Claire. The list is composed of all of the things that she is unable to do the things that her friends do and that she feels she should be able to do. One of the rules that she challenges is her bedtime of 9:30. In response to her complaints, they allow Rudy to stay up as late as she wants to as long as she does all of her homework, get herself up in the mornings and she cannot be late to school, even once.

The first night they allow her stay up late, she stays up all night long. When it's time for her to get up in the morning, she is unable to wake herself up. When Cliff goes in to wake her, she doesn't want to get up for school due to exhaustion. Despite this, Rudy still has to go to school.

BEFORE SHE ARRIVES HOME, her teacher calls home and tells Cliff that she was very irritable throughout the day and unable to focus on her classwork. When she gets home and is asked about how she's feeling and how her day went, she says that she is not tired and felt even smarter in school—most likely due to her staying up late at night.

VANESSA GOES into her room while she is doing her homework to congratulate her on getting her parents to allow her to stay up past her bedtime… something she had also tried to do but had been unsuccessful at when she was Rudy's age. However, instead of Rudy taking it as a compliment, she is paranoid, feeling that Vanessa is making fun of her because she is tired. That night, she is invited by Cliff to stay up late with him and watch TV. As soon as she gets downstairs and the show starts, she is asleep.

THAT'S us as adults as well. We don't know the value of rest. Like infants going through a sleep regression, we're fighting to stay awake out of fear that we are missing out on something if we take the time to rest.

I, too, struggled with this rule when I was a child. I wanted to stay up late and watch TV or read… anything to not have to go to sleep. Now, as an adult, I see exactly what the adults saw; they were speaking from experience. It's so hard to perform at my greatest capacity without having a good night's rest.

HOWEVER, contrary to this knowledge, it seems like the older that I get, the more work I have to complete and the less time there is for me to sleep. It's crazy how the first thing I sacrifice is sleep even knowing what I know, right? I know that I cannot be the only person who does this. Can I?

WHEN TASKED with trying to fit everything into my day, the first thing I always think to give up is sleep. However, I'm quickly learning that it is counterproductive for me to skip sleep to complete work.

THINKING BACK on all of the times when I have missed sleep to cram in work, I went to work the next day only a shell of the person that I typically am. I would be forgetful, moving in slow motion and mad at the world. Snapping at people for saying good morning and using the excuse that I wasn't a morning person when the reality was that I hadn't gotten enough sleep the night before. I've also suffered from sleep deprivation headaches a time or two or three.

OUTSIDE OF THESE THINGS, not getting enough sleep can cause your immune system to weaken, you to gain weight, and even affect the way that you look if you continuously don't get enough sleep. Rest is an important part of anything that you are creating. Not only does rest prevent getting burned out, it also provides you with the opportunity to connect back to yourself and your needs through self-care which in turn allows you to actually show up in all of the areas of your life.

FOR SOME REASON, rest is frowned upon in this current generation. People believe that rest means that you aren't working or that you are lazy when that is the furthest from the truth. This rhetoric is even being spewed to the younger generation in songs and quotes on clothes, etc. One quote that I've seen from time to time and heard just as much is "no days off".

. . .

I USED to spew that rhetoric as well not realizing how I was playing myself. Like many people, I took pride in saying 'no days off' like it gave me a badge of honor or something. Well, I'm here to tell you that it doesn't.

I LEARNED from one of my leaders that there is no medal of honor for the person that can work the greatest number of hours. The only reward you will receive from overworking yourself and not getting any sleep is bags under your eyes, adding a few more years onto your appearance, irritability and exhaustion.

REST IS REQUIRED to be productive. It gives you an opportunity to self-evaluate, allowing for clearer points of views. It aids in reducing stress, increasing alertness, restoring depleted energy and recharging your mental battery by rejuvenating you and giving you the ability to start fresh.

REST IS ESPECIALLY important if you're in leadership; you can't effectively lead if you're tired. I can remember working a solid 28 hours straight. Sure, it was productive, and a lot of work got done during that time but, when it was over, so was I. My body checked out on me, and I was useless for the next 48 hours because exhaustion set in.

So, technically, all of the work that I put in was really those two days' worth of work. Furthermore, those two days of work that I crammed into one shift took it's time back with the sleep that I got over the course of the two days that I was out of commission. So, was it really worth it?

Not resting can result in the inability to focus and concentrate on your goal. It also causes you to make mistakes that you wouldn't normally make had you gotten rest. For instance, have you ever crammed for an exam, pulling an all nighter and then when it was time for you to take the exam, you couldn't remember the answer to some of the easiest questions? That is from the sleep deprivation.

Now, if you have been depriving yourself of sleep for a long time and you need help getting your sleep schedule back on track, I can help you with that. Here are some suggestions on how you can sleep schedule back on track.

. . .

Use your smartphone. If you have an iPhone, the Health app has a sleep section that allows you to input your sleep schedule. This includes when you would like to wake up and how much sleep you would like to get each night. Once you've inserted this information, the app will tell you what time you need to go to sleep each night in order to achieve that amount of sleep. The app also puts your phone in Do Not Disturb mode so that if phone calls, text messages or other notifications come into your phone, they won't bother you.

This is beneficial because most people are so into their phones that they can't get to sleep when it's time to. Studies have also found that the blue light that comes from your devices reduces the melatonin hormone that triggers sleep.

Don't do any work after a certain time. The later you work, the more wired you are. Seriously, working stimulates you. It also puts you into an alert state and when you work late into the day/afternoon, instead of your body winding down and relaxing in preparation for sleep, it is stimulated, focusing on work. Therefore, don't do any tasks after a certain time. Make sure to give yourself ample time to relax before bedtime to make sure that you get a good night's sleep.

. . .

STOP THINKING that not sleeping equates to productivity. It is detrimental to your mood, memory, focus and more to skip sleep. And if you are skipping sleep in an effort to get more work done, then keep in mind that the two will cancel each other out at some point. Remember my example up above. You may get more work done now, but when your body is playing catch up with sleep later, you'll be getting more rest and no work done. There is no way around it.

IF THESE SUGGESTIONS don't help you with getting your sleep schedule back on track, just remember that time off is necessary; we should not normalize working extreme hours. When you get enough sleep, everything else in your life will be better. Including your health as well as your mental health, your clarity, creativity and mood. Don't believe me? Give it a try. Tell me how it works out for you.

5

SELF-ACCOUNTABILITY

Ac·count·a·bil·i·ty
/əˌkoun(t)əˈbilədē/

noun

1. the fact or condition of being accountable; responsibility.

In high school, I fretted having to work with a group for more reasons than one. The main reason though was that I didn't want to be held accountable for everyone else's work. It was one thing to be held accountable for my own work but having to be accountable for someone else's? That was where I drew the line.

. . .

As I got older though, I realized that there was beauty to working with others. Many times, we feel that we don't need accountability partners. Why would we need anyone else to hold us accountable for our actions, or lack of… we can do that ourselves, right? But do we, really? When you don't follow through with your plans or take the necessary actions to achieve your goals, what happens? Maybe an accountability partner isn't what you need and instead, what you do need is to develop your self-accountability, after-all. I'm going to help you with that.

Self accountability or personal accountability, as some people refer to it, is essential when it comes to being successful and improving your life. To me, it's the act of *'starting with the man in the mirror'* and realizing that in order to see real change, it has to start with you. Morally, self-accountability should be the most important thing to you.

Why? Because if you continuously blame your failures or issues, regardless of how big or small, personal or work related—on other people, circumstances beyond your control, or just plain bad luck, you will fail.

. . .

One thing that I truly despise is people who make excuses for why they aren't where they feel they should be in their lives. I'm sure you know someone like that… we all do, don't we? Those are the people who love to blame their failures and mishaps on others but will claim their successes for themselves. How is that? The reality is that there are no excuses when it comes to your success. You are responsible for your success, whether you want to believe it or not.

Especially grown adults who had the free will to make the decisions that lead them to where they currently are in their lives, but they are putting the blame on everyone else. Remember, the life that you are living is your own… no one else's. The thoughts that go through your mind, your actions, decisions and behaviors—they all belong to you.

Most times, our setbacks are self-inflicted, and we don't have the courage to hold our own selves accountable. It's very easy to blame others for our downfalls but it's extremely hard to do a self-assessment and ask yourself what is it that you could have done differently.

. . .

I'VE SEEN people that have terrible experiences at restaurants; the food was not great, and the service was not good. Those people can't wait to hold the restaurant and its staff accountable. However, let them cook for someone and the food don't come out the way that they expected it to, and it'll be everyone else's fault… including the kitchen sink.

SELF-ACCOUNTABILITY IS a mindset that more people should learn and adapt to. Even deeper, self-accountability is a way of thinking and being, it's a lifestyle that people should embrace instead of shying away from.

SOME THINGS that you can adapt to in order to hold yourself accountable would be:

REMAINING TRUTHFUL, always. Lying about your mistake or putting the blame on someone else keeps you in a place of, should I say, comfort. You'll never grow and learn if you don't tell the truth.

HOLDING YOURSELF ACCOUNTABLE, even when no one is looking. Sometimes, we make mistakes that only we know about. The true test is whether we remain honest to ourselves. If a choice you made didn't pan out the way you expected it to, don't blame someone else. Acknowledge that you made a mistake, now how can you fix it? Remember, if a tree falls in the woods when no one is around, it still makes a sound.

Always get clarity. Sometimes, mistakes arise because we aren't sure about what is expected of us. Therefore, always double and triple check everything. Even ensure that you have it in writing, this way, you can always go back to what was expected and there will be no room for you to miss a thing.

Acknowledge how powerful being responsible is. Don't just take responsibility for the good things… the bad things need someone to take responsibility for them too. The beauty of taking responsibility either way is that you have the opportunity to learn if it didn't work out. It's also empowering to own responsibility… no could have, would haves or should haves… only what is.

Take some action every day toward your goals and monitor your progress in a journal, planner, or some other written means. Procrastination occurs when we are overwhelmed or in belief that we are going to fail. That is what prevents us from making things happen. Repeat after me… I will not fail. I will not lose. Now, get out there and start attacking your plans little by little. Be sure to monitor your progress as well. The best way to evaluate yourself and what you have done or have not done is to write things down this way you can always return to it and see what has been done or what needs to be done as well as what has worked and what needs to be adjusted.

Your accountability to yourself should supersede your accountability to others. Do you value others more than you value yourself? Then you should not ever consider the accountability for someone else over your accountability to yourself. At the end of the day, you have to live with you. Your success, your progress, your failures and mishaps should all be at the top of your totem pole. If you aren't pleased with yourself, what else matters? When you hold yourself accountable for the results you need to produce, no one else will ever have to. This is the mindset of personal leadership, and it undergirds your success and your productivity.

Don't be too hard on yourself. When things don't work out as planned, ad lib or redirect. It's good to not shelter yourself. You can gain knowledge from others around you. This chapter coincides with failure and planning.

Keep in mind, there is growth in self accountability. A lot of times, you'll discover something that you didn't know about yourself or your ability to do something when you are holding yourself accountable. It may not feel good but it's being acknowledged and with self accountability, it's also being addressed.

The more accountable you are, the more you will succeed. Again, accountability opens the door for growth and more knowledge. You cannot learn something that you already know. So, don't be afraid to take ownership of your mistakes. The knowledge you receive from it will thank you!

6

LISTEN

Lis·ten

/ˈlis(ə)n/

verb

1. give one's attention to a sound.

'THERE IS SO MUCH *that you can learn when you just listen!'* Have you ever heard that saying before? Well, I have. More times than I could count actually. The funny thing is that it applies to the majority of us.

. . .

It doesn't matter what industry you are a part of or planning to join, as a leader, sooner or later everything that you do will rely on the interpersonal relationships that you form with your team, stakeholders, customers and more. In order to build relationships with these people, active listening is a must. Otherwise, you'll have a harder time building the relationships with them if you don't understand the problems at hand or if you aren't able to acknowledge them in a positive, reassuring way.

Having a lack of understanding of the problems can also translate to difficulty getting to the root of an issue as well as trouble analyzing for and developing inventive and original solutions. All of these things can make those around you question whether you are really qualified to be the leader and in the worst-case scenario, it can lead to problems like insubordination, low morale, poor productivity and barbaric retention rates. In the retrospect, this will cut your ability to compete and keep the doors of your company (or the company that you are representing for) open.

There's a saying that goes, you were given two ears and one mouth so that you can listen twice as much as you speak. I wholeheartedly believe this and try to live by it as well. The importance of listening gets overlooked a lot of the time. But not listening can cause us to miss out on important things because we have failed to take heed.

For starters, listening is the most crucial part of communication and a very pertinent aspect of success. Every idea comes from information, whether you get it from someone or from God. In order to receive the information, you have to be a good listener. Not just to what you want to hear and what agrees with your narrative but things that don't always suit your narrative or goals as well.

This can be challenging though when you consider the fact that we are in a new age. Communication when I was younger was a conversation, face to face or over the phone. We even wrote letters and sent postcards also. Now, conversations take place via text message, social media and emails. Due to the shift in how we communicate, there is also starting to be a shift in how we listen. Needless to say, a lot of people are losing the ability to listen.

. . .

One of the main reasons that people miss vital information is because they aren't listening. And when I say that they aren't listening, I mean that they are not *actively* listening. What they are doing instead is listening without paying attention or they're listening to respond/hearing what is being said but not comprehending it.

Many of us are guilty of hearing opposed to listening. The difference? One is physical—hearing and one is mental—listening. The latter requires you to process the information you receive which in turn will allow you to understand it. While the first one will literally go in one ear and out the other if you aren't careful.

Another way that I like to decipher between the two… hearing is like when you're driving and you've zoned out. When you finally reach your destination, you don't recall a thing about the drive… you don't even know how you made it there. Listening is like learning a new dance move, you have to be focused, engaged and purposeful to achieve or master it.

It's important to be a good listener in order to stay on top of the details. Regardless of the position that you hold, being a good listener is the difference between being successful and being a failure.

In order to be a good listener, you have to remain unbiased, nonjudgmental and attentive—actively paying attention to verbal and nonverbal cues, among other things. You also have to let go of assumptions… you know what they say about assuming; you make a fool out of yourself. You also need to care about what the people you are listening to have to say and seeing the value in them and their words.

Listening is very important in success but especially important throughout life. By being a good listener, you become a good/better person to those around you—including those who mean the most to you. You also will always know what those around you want, supply and demand. Another reason listening is important is because it can prevent you from making mistakes and encountering things that are not conducive to your success.

The good thing though, all isn't lost if you are not a good listener. Here are some ways you can improve this skill:

. . .

Find distraction free places to have your conversations. Sometimes, we aren't good listeners not because we don't want to be but because there is so much going on around us that it is impossible to not pay attention to the commotion of the world. If you are serious about the conversation that you are planning to have and you want to retain the information, find somewhere quiet to have the conversation.

Pay attention. Sounds easy, right? It can be if you simply tune out all of the outside noises and give your undivided attention to the person with the floor.

Show that you are interested in what the speaker is talking about. I don't know about anyone else, but I know that I can always tell when someone is listening to me. I look for signs like eye contact, nodding and the occasional "uh huh".

Allow the individual who is talking to complete their statement/ or thought. The only way that you can respond as necessary to the statements or thoughts if it is necessary is if you have heard the entire message. If you respond too prematurely, without allowing the speaker to complete their thought, then you are reacting or responding to an incomplete thought. Who knows? Maybe you're wasting your breath… they may have had the same exact thought as you. You would have known that though if you'd let them finish.

REPHRASE what was said to you using your own words. This will help you to ensure that not only were you listening, but you comprehend what has been said to you. This is often the part that a lot of people get stumped on. Comprehending is the most important part of listening. This includes recognizing speech sounds, understanding the meaning of individual words, and/or understanding the syntax of sentences in which they are presented.

A QUOTE I that I love is *'learn from the mistakes (advice) of others, you don't live long enough to make them all on your own.'* People that have been where you are and people that are where you are trying to go, may know some things that can help you. When you don't listen, you are subjecting yourself to unnecessary road-blocks, potholes and in some cases, sinking holes.

. . .

Being able to listen to others gives you high yielding results in your work and better relationships with those around you. By improving your listening skills, you improve your ability to succeed and your level of success, as well as your self-accountability, and more.

7

COMPLACENCY

Com·pla·cen·cy
/kəmˈplāsənsē/

NOUN

1. a feeling of smug or uncritical satisfaction with oneself or one's achievements.

- Side note: This is a chapter that I believe coincides with failure. When you fail, you continue to work towards fixing the problem and achieving the goal. Well, complacency is the opposite. It's when you've reached some kind of success and in turn, you don't believe that you need to improve.

I CAN RECALL hearing 'if it ain't broke, don't fix it' in relation to success. In other words, you already have it right, why change it? That's a problem… you never know how much better you can be if you stop trying.

THIS IS a common issue among leaders and businesses. Many people have a reactive response to this. Only after they've seen a dip in sales do they bother to try to find out what is wrong and how they can fix it. When everything is going good though, they go with the flow, never once thinking about how they can improve their business.

WHILE RESEARCHING FOR THIS CHAPTER, I came across a blog that spoke about Kodak and how their complacency killed their business. They were so stuck on the production of film and disposable cameras that although they were the creator of the digital camera, they allowed other companies to come in and surpass them because they were still so stuck on what had created their success for them—the disposable film and camera.

. . .

For people who experience success, sometimes they get so stuck on what worked for them and the way that they reached success that they fail to evolve beyond that point. This leads to them getting left behind while the rest of their competitors excel.

Complacency is a form of satisfaction. Self-satisfaction. It's the act of being content with your current situation that you fail to try harder for more. It's the act of becoming comfortable, or lazy depending on who you ask. Complacency is not having a desire to improve yourself… being comfortable with whatever progress you've made so far.

Think about it, when was the last time you thought to yourself, this is good. Let me figure out how I can make it better. Never, right?

I know someone who started a business not too long ago making desserts. Their most popular dessert was a vegan banana pudding. The pudding was good… so good, people were paying $1.00 an ounce just about. Needless to say, the creator of the pudding became complacent with that recipe. Despite the fact that a few people were telling her that her pudding was too sweet and had too many cookies, she saw how much money she was pulling in and never once bothered to make any of the suggested suggestions. She never even tried them out. Instead, she allowed business to carry on until it was pretty much non-existent.

By the time she was just about out of customers, she decided that it wouldn't hurt to try out the changes that had been suggested to her. But at that time, there was no one around to give it a try.

Complacency is feeling like you are in a good place therefore, you don't need to challenge or outdo yourself. Complacency occurs when you stop reflecting on your success and experiences. Once you stop reflecting on your success and trying to better yourself, you stop trying to achieve the next step of your goal. One thing I always knew growing up is that I never wanted to be comfortable… I never wanted to be complacent. I always wanted to strive for more, even when I was tired and I couldn't quite put my finger on what more was. I knew that I wanted it.

. . .

THIS IS one of the biggest character flaws of a lot of people that prevents them from being successful— their complacency. Dave Stutman said that complacency was the enemy of success, and he was absolutely correct.

COMPLACENCY AND SUCCESS cannot coexist although they do, many times. For one to thrive, the other must take a back seat. If you allow complacency to thrive, you are allowing contentment, laziness and more to thrive in your life. Among many things, complacency stunts growth and ultimately leads to your demise.

HOWEVER, growth can be hard when you aren't getting enough of what you need to thrive. For some reason, this makes me think about knockout roses (one of my favorite flowers). They are versatile flowers as they can grow in the pot or in the yard but in order to grow, they are required to have 8-10 hours of sunlight. They cannot be over or under fed with fertilizer and they must be well watered but cannot be drowned either.

HERE ARE some strategies you can adopt in order to keep complacency from robbing you of your ability to grow.

. . .

Set ambitious goals and do everything in your power to achieve it. If you're not setting gigantic goals and achieving them, or if your goals aren't surpassing your abilities then you need to set bigger goals. Compete against your own track record—remember, your only competition is yourself. Whatever you need to do in order to set higher goals should be done, even if you need to change the way that you measure success altogether.

If you are in a role of leadership, the people around you will welcome and appreciate the challenges—well, for the most part that is. In fact, challenging your team is more than likely to make them more engaged and productive. It'll keep them on their feet learning and doing new things as time passes them by.

Do some research. If you were to ask your loyal, long-term clients why they do business with you, what do you think that they would say? Maybe do an anonymous poll or putting up a feedback box so that your customer can provide you with feedback. Feedback is the mother of improvement. The more you know, the better you will be able to meet prospects' and clients' needs in the future.

. . .

Ask your peers and team what they think. Besides you, who knows your business the best? The people who work for and/or with you. With that in mind, know that no one is committed to your success like those individuals. Let your team know that you want to get in front of the next big innovation and lead it, not follow it. Get input from the people that you respect and admire as well. Have roundtable talks and ask everyone to give their opinions and feedback on what can be done to improve the processes that they work with every day. By getting their opinion, you will hear about improvements that only those on the front lines of client service and case design are aware of.

Get out of your comfort zone. Let me tell you a secret being comfortable does **not** align with being innovative and creative. What can be done while in your comfort zone that can to push you and your team beyond what's comfortable and familiar? Is there a revenue stream, a demographic market or some other "next step" you've been avoiding because it seems complicated or unfamiliar? That's exactly the direction that you need to move in to otherwise, you'll never grown. an area you need to consider moving into.

. . .

Reassess everything. When was the last time that you assessed your goals and plans? When was the last time that you tried something new? The thought is that you can learn something new only when you approach topics — even those you know a lot about — like a true beginner. You try to see what you know so well with fresh eyes and a new perspective.

Be mindful that he same way that you have to adjust how you care for the knockout roses in order to ensure that they grow to their fullest potential, is the same way that you have to adjust with yourself to ensure that you reach your fullest potential.

8

MENTORSHIP

Men·tor·ship
/ˈmentôrSHip,ˈmentərSHip/

NOUN

1. the guidance provided by a mentor, especially an experienced person in a company or educational institution.

We don't place enough value on mentorship.

. . .

Regardless of what your profession or goal is, you should have a mentor. There should always be someone around you who is more advanced than you are in your profession that can provide you with the necessary guidance upon reaching or receiving your goal.

There are a multitude of benefits when it comes to mentoring. Studies show that having a good mentor has the ability to lead to greater career success, including promotions, raises, and increased opportunities. For the companies that embrace mentoring, they are rewarded with higher levels of employee engagement, retention, and knowledge sharing.

A mentor is a supportive professional who helps to guide a lesser experienced person in their professional endeavors with their acquired expertise, wisdom and knowledge. Have you ever heard the quote, 'hindsight is 20/20'? Well, that's the power of a mentor. You are their hindsight therefore, the things they wish someone would have told them, they can now tell you. The person you choose to be your mentor should be very supportive and have your best interest at heart.

. . .

Effective mentoring takes a lot of effort, skill and structure from both the mentor and the mentee. In order for the relationship to be successful and for the mentee to experience success, both parties have to take responsibility for making it work.

When done right, mentorships can increase confidence, bring forth a higher self awareness. It can lead to promotions and a bigger and better personal network. It is also an effective way to share knowledge, increase engagement and retention and recruit new staff in organizations that enlist a mentoring program.

Mentoring relationships are extremely important. I believe a mentor should be one that can help to guide you along your journey on the road to success. They should also be engaged in your success, wanting the best for you as they do for themselves. A mentor in my opinion does not have to be a friend, although I think if a friendship is formed between you and your mentor, it makes the relationship better. However, they should definitely be someone that will comfortably give you the unvarnished truth about yourself.

. . .

HAVING a mentor means getting raw feedback that may sting. Despite that, it is necessary and pertinent to your success. That's how you grow. It's also how you see yourself and reflect. There is this model called the Johari Window. It has four windows; two which are known to yourself and two which are not known to yourself. Simultaneously, two of the windows are known to others and two of them are not known to others. The four windows are called: the open area, the blind spot, the hidden area and the unknown.

MENTORSHIPS EXPOSE THE BLIND SPOT. The things that are known to outsiders but not known to yourself. If done right and both parties are open to it, mentorships can enhance your personality through feedback, disclosure and perception.

EVEN WITH ALL of the benefits of having a mentor, there are times when mentorships do not work. For starters, if you are being forced into a mentorship opposed to taking on the responsibility because it is something that you wish to participate in. Many colleges and companies assign leaders as mentors. The problem with that is that they don't take into consideration what the mentor may already have on their plate. They also don't consider if its something that the mentor wants to do. As we all know, when you are not fond of doing something, it shows in your actions. Being assigned a mentor who is busy, not interested, incompetent or dysfunctional will never be beneficial to either party involved.

UNDERSTAND that mentorships should also have obligations that are required by both the mentor and you, the mentee. I remember having a mentor that was assigned to me. This mentorship started off great. The person assigned to be my mentor began our mentorship by sending me a book in the mail. I was so excited to begin the relationship, receive the book and begin reading it! Unfortunately, although this mentor had great intentions, they committed at a time when they really could not do it.

MENTORSHIP IS A HIGHLY rewarding experience for both the mentor and the mentee, but in order for either party to receive all of the benefits of the relationship, they must both be committed to the mentorship. They need to make time for one another, be great listeners, personable, honest and open to constructive criticism and learning from one another.

. . .

THE MENTOR that I was assigned had more responsibilities than they realized, and it led to them not having the time necessary to dedicate to my growth and development. They failed to join a zoom call that was scheduled for us one day. Due to that, I fired the mentor.

IF A MENTOR that you select or that is selected for you doesn't fit, you can fire that mentor and start over. They are humans too and may have an overwhelming life and that's okay; if they can't commit, move on. The best mentors are going to be honest with you.

I REMEMBER HAVING another mentor and when we decided to start our mentorship, he was very attentive. He listened as I shared my dreams, my goals and my aspirations. Afterwards, do you know what he told me? He told me that I needed to dream bigger! That scared me because I didn't believe in myself enough to dream bigger at that moment. However, that right there is exactly why mentors are needed and great.

THEY CAN SEE in you what you cannot see in yourself. Had it not been for my mentor, I would have still been dreaming mediocre. Today, because of the belief that my mentor had in me, the correction that he provided me and the value that he placed on me, I'm doing something that I never dreamed of.

If you ever decide to be a mentor or a mentee, here are a few tips that you should consider in order to ensure that you are having a fulfilling mentorship.

Be open to feedback. Regardless of what role you are in, you should always be open to feedback. Feedback promotes personal and professional enhancement. When you are open to it, you can learn from it. Remember, it doesn't matter who the teacher is, if the information being given is important, then we should be open to it and accepting of it.

Share sufficient and pertinent information. If you are going to be a mentor, you should have the knowledge on whatever topic you are being asked to mentor on. You should also be willing to share it. Knowledge is power but that power must be shared. Hoarding knowledge will not make you anymore successful and it surely will not be beneficial to your mentee.

. . .

Reach out and stay in touch. You should try reaching out to your mentor at least once a month… maybe once every other month, just to check in and see how they are. Too often, people lose touch with one another. The downside to this is that you never know what could have come from a continued relationship with your mentor or mentee. You never know… maybe one day they will be able to connect you to your dream job, give you important career advice or write you a bomb letter of recommendation.

Have realistic goals/requirements. Having unrealistic goals and expectations of your mentorship is the quickest way to send it to the dumpster. What you are expecting of your mentor, they should be able to expect of you. Remember, mentorships do not provide the mentor with incentives. Therefore, you cannot expect them to be on call 24/7 for you. Be reasonable with what you are requiring from your mentorship. I promise, it'll work out for the best.

Follow up. Always circle back and follow up with your mentor or mentee. Sometimes, life can be overwhelming… it doesn't matter who you are. For that reason, you should always follow up with your mentor or mentee. If you are the mentee, be sure to inform your mentor how their advice worked out or how the job interview that you guys talked about went. If you are the mentor, take a moment to ask what the results were from a conversation you told your mentee to have. This is an essential aspect of any relationship but especially a mentorship.

Stay motivated. I think this one is pretty self explanatory. If you start consistent, remain consistent throughout the entire mentorship. There is nothing worse than someone who dwindles in the midst of the mentorship. Remain motivated and watch how your relationship can flourish!

Overall, being mentored by the right person can prove to be very beneficial. As we discussed above, mentoring —when done right—can encourage you and empower you in your personal life as well as in your career. It can help you to identify and achieve career goals and help you to identify and correct gaps in generic skills and knowledge. Beyond that, mentoring also gives you the ability to dream bigger.

9

PATIENCE

Pa·tience
/ˈpāSHəns/

NOUN

THE CAPACITY TO accept or tolerate delay, trouble, or suffering without getting angry or upset.

I REMEMBER HEARING a bunch of quotes growing up in relation to patience. Everything from, "Patience is a virtue" to "The day that you plant the seed is not the same day that you eat the fruit." My favorite patience quote though is, "Patience is not simply the ability to wait - it's how we behave while we're waiting" by Joyce Meyer.

HER QUOTE IS my favorite because despite it not feeling like it, patience is an act of self control. When we act impulsively, a lot of the time, the consequences outweigh the reward. Success begins with patience whether we know it or not. Patience and the commitment to put in the work needed for your success. However, patience is not easy to come by.

NOT MANY OF us have the patience to see the things that we aspire to do and become through. Many of us don't even have patience with ourselves.

YET PATIENCE IS the one morality that serves us well. It takes time and a conscious effort to master, but lack of patience can lead to our demise. Depending on who you ask, patience may be one of the most underrated attributes of success. A lot of times, we are in a rush to become successful. We see how it is happening for those around us and it makes us anxious to see our own success come to life.

. . .

We don't realize that for those around us, they may have been on the road to their success for months or years prior. We just see the end result and not the process and believe that it should be that "easy" for us.

Especially with social media being a factor. We are currently living in a world of immediacy. We all have smart phones and know what everyone is doing every second of everyday because they keep us informed with Facebook, Instagram, Snapchat and other social sites that allows people to update the world on their movements. Due to this, we are conditioned to believe that if we have to wait, something is wrong.

Think about it. How many times have you tried opening a web page or application on your phone and it took too long to open? What is the first thing that you thought of? Something was wrong with your service? Right? Exactly. Instant gratification has taken over our lives and given us timeframes and deadlines that many of us cannot live up to. We want results immediately. This applies to every aspect of our lives being that we now have access to the internet 24/7 in the palms of our hands.

. . .

THEREFORE, instead of going through the process of writing out your goals, planning, doing the work and more, we rush the process. Then, we get discouraged when we don't get the results that we set our hearts on. The truth is though that there is a lot of work, time and patience that goes into being successful. Sometimes, it can even take years of patience and hard work before you start to see the rewards from it.

A FEW YEARS AGO, there was a weight gain fad called Apetamin. It is a liquid vitamin that causes people who struggle to gain weight, or want to gain weight, do so fast. Apetamin is a syrup that is made in Indian and considered unsafe in America due to one of the ingredients in it which is only assessable in the United States by prescription.

APETAMIN WORKS by increasing your appetite and making you sleep as well. Some people have gained as much as twenty to twenty-five pounds in a month. However, for most people, the moment you stop taking the Apetamin, you lose all of the weight you gained while on it. Other than losing the weight just as quickly as you gain it, there are a lot of side effects that can consume you. Extreme drowsiness, kidney problems, liver disease, swelling of your feet and ankles, vomiting and blurred vision are just a few of the side effects that you may encounter.

THIS GOES to show you what can happen when you do not have patience and look for a "get rich quick" scheme. There is the possibility that you will lose it just as fast as you gain it and there is also the possibility that it will hurt you more than it helps you.

IT'S NOT uncommon to feel that being patient has you at a standstill. However, being patient is everything but that. Patience allows you the opportunity to see the bigger picture. Is this something that you really want? Be patient and stay the course. If you work towards what it is that you want and stay diligent, it'll come. But only when it is God's tine and not on your timing.

EMBRACING patience can aid you in becoming a better person by avoiding being forced to make a hasty decision. It allows you to remain calm and composed and think things out. In order to become a master of anything you must have patience. That is the only way that you can develop your inborn abilities and talents… by making a continued effort to enhance or perfect your talent over time.

. . .

I WENT through a period where I questioned myself regarding my value, worth and ability due to not moving along the success train at the speed that I believed that I should. There were so many people around me that were getting promoted and I wasn't. Even down to individuals who had less tenure than me and yet, they were moving on to bigger things while I stayed idle. I felt stuck. I was so discouraged. I had to learn that the journey to success for everyone is different.

WE COMPARE ourselves from one view which is our current situation and other peoples' glory. We see the glory and the success for others, but we don't see the blood, the sweat, the tears, the grind and the grit behind the scenes. We don't see what they went through before the elevation.

IN ORDER TO develop your patience, here are a few things that I believe you can do.

MAKE Yourself Wait. This is the best way to build patience by yourself, for yourself. Have you ever walked in the store and seen something that you wanted and had to have it, right that moment? We're all guilty of it. Next time though, don't purchase it right away. Give yourself a day or two before purchasing it, who knows... maybe you won't even want it when you go back for it. Besides, if it is there, you may not even want it anymore. You just might realize that there is no reason to purchase it after all.

Complete a puzzle or two. Want to know something that really requires patience? Try completing a hard Sudoku or a crossword. You'll be sitting there all day. If you really want to know what patience is, pull out a puzzle. You may be completing it for a few days but by the time you finish, you'll be well acquainted with patience.

Read a book. There are very few people who actually take the time necessary to actually *read* a book. Most people would rather pay Audible a few dollars a month to get credits and listen to someone read the book to them. Not only will reading a book provide you with patience, but it will also award you with focus and control along with it.

. . .

Take public transportation more often. I love a good train or bus ride. Why? Well for starters, outside of patience—waiting for the bus or train and making stops along the route—it also forces you to remove your expectations. Being that you are not the driver, taking public transportation affords someone else the control of your departure and arrival.

Stop watching the time on your cell phone. When I was a child, my parents made sure to let me know that the more I watched the clock, the slower it would tick. They were right. On days when I am ready to get clocked out of work so that I can hurry up and get home are the days when the clock moves even slower than it normally does. Clock watching is sure to make you more impatient than anything.

Pay attention to what makes you impatient. Does not leaving early enough for work or an appointment make you more impatient than usual? If so, and you've been paying attention to that then you now know what you need to do in order to take control over that feeling of impatience. By paying attention to what makes you impatient, you can take actions to alleviate that stress from your life.

. . .

Meditate. Breathe. Feel yourself relax. Now, focus on your next breath and releasing any emotions that do not serve you. Especially impatience.

Give yourself a time out. Sometimes, taking a minute to yourself—going for a walk or whatever else you'd like to do while on your break is enough to help you clear your head and then come back with a relaced spirit.

Accept the things in which you cannot change. God, grant me the serenity to accept the things I cannot change, courage to change the things I can, and wisdom to know the difference. Somethings aren't even worth the uproar that it will cause, especially those things that you cannot change. Acknowledge when you cannot change something and accept it.

Lastly, trust yourself and your process. There will be times where no matter what you do to avoid it, something will happen that will spark your impatience and frustration. That's fine. Allow yourself to be impatient sometimes. It's all apart of the process.

10

UNDERSTAND YOUR PURPOSE

Pur·pose

/ˈpərpəs/

NOUN

1. the reason for which something is done or created or for which something exists.

IN A FEW CHAPTERS, you're going to read about authenticity. This is the prerequisite of it. The first step to being authentic is to embrace your true self. Go beyond what others think and look deep within yourself. The truth is, we are all on this earth for a deep and specific reason, and to understand what that deeper reason is simply begins with purpose.

Purpose is where your life finds meaning. It's the reason why you made this trip to earth… to supply the world with your purpose. It keeps you centered, focused and clear on what really matters to you and what you want out of life. Simply put, purpose aligns what you do with who you are.

Having a crystal-clear idea of your purpose empowers you to put your attention and actions on the things that matter the most to you. It forces you to take risks regardless of any odds or obstacles that may be stacked against you. It is the drive, the determination and the reserve of energy that you didn't know you had.

So, what is your purpose? Have you ever really sat down and thought about what makes your life worth living? What makes you the happiest? What will make work feel like fun for you? If not, then you need to get to it.

. . .

Most people believe that your purpose is already inside of you, waiting for you to figure it out. If you go to Google and type into the search bar 'How to find my purpose', you'll find numerous quizzes and self-help books that are supposedly able to help you uncover your purpose.

Some people are aware of their passions and life missions from the time that they are born and remain true to it, not allowing others to sway them with their opinions and beliefs. As children, we haven't been indoctrinated yet. So, life for us is free. We are free to access our passions and purpose without being shaped by worldly experiences and needing money. Then on the other side of the spectrum, some people knew what they were passionate about as children but lost it and now, the process is taking much longer than they expected to figure out what it is they are meant to be doing.

We all have a purpose, some of us make it our mission to tap into it and some of become complacent with making a living and surviving that we fail to find out what our life's purpose may be. For those who don't figure out their purpose and act on it, they spend their lives in misery because they've stifled their true voice... their true wants and true desires.

. . .

When it was time to graduate high school and go into the "real world" as most people call it, this was something I was plagued with, like many high school students are. What did I want to be? Who did I want to be? What did I love? What would make me happy to do every day without feeling like I was sacrificing myself in order to live? What did the world need that only I could provide? What was I good at?

I had no idea. Well, maybe I did have an idea but instead, I did what most people do and went with what the teachers and other adults in my life were telling me to do. I based my decision on what would allow me to make a good living. What profession could I go into that would pay me good money? That's what a lot of people do instead of really getting to know themselves and listening to what their heart is telling them to do.

That led to me changing jobs a few times until I found one that I could stomach for a while. Then, when I could no longer stomach that one, I left it for the career that I really loved. My purpose has always been present. It's always been the thing that made me the happiest.

. . .

YOUR PURPOSE IS DIRECTLY ALIGNED with your success. Actually, your success begins with your purpose. Where do your skills, interests, talents and desires meet?

YOUR PURPOSE IS what brings you gratification in life and what makes you happy. The line of work that I am in requires a passion for people and customer service. This is not a profession that you should enter if you are not a people person. If you are working in an environment where it is people driven or people focused and you don't "like people", you will never find success. It doesn't matter how you slice the pie; you will never be happy. If you're going to work and it brings you joy, that means you're passionate about what you do.

IF YOU DON'T KNOW what your purpose in life is yet, I need to know... do you *want* to know what your purpose is? If so, there are a few steps you can take to figure it out. Start by :

EMBRACING YOUR TRUE SELF. What others think and feel doesn't matter. All that matters is what you think and feel.

. . .

Exploring your interest. What do you love to do? If you had nothing else to do, what would you do all day? What comes easy to you and feel natural?

Create a mission statement for your life. What would your life reflect if you were operating in your highest vision? What would you be doing? What would you have? Where would you be? Combine those all in your life's mission statement, now, you have a clearer idea of what your purpose is.

Listen to your heart. A busy and stressful life prevents you from hearing and listening to your heart. Your heart sends you messages daily, however, we get stuck in the hustle and bustle of life and most times, we can't hear it. In order to hear what your heart has to say, you have to provide the right atmosphere. Block out a time on your planner each day where you can take time for yourself. Sit quietly with yourself and write out anything you feel that you need to.

Next, ask yourself these questions:

. . .

What did you love to do as a child before life (and the adults around you) told you to get practical?

What would you be doing if money was not an issue?

What makes you forget about the world around you?

What makes you happiest? What makes you feel alive?

What would you do if you knew you couldn't fail?

What would you like to be remembered for in death?

Be sure to give yourself space to really think about these questions before you respond to them. Also, keep in mind that everything is doable. Maybe to outsiders, they'll tell you that your dreams are outlandish, but these are your dreams and goals. They can't phantom your view because they weren't given the vision. It's all yours.

Whatever your answer was to those questions... well, that is your passion. That is the driving force behind who you are and what you love.

Be mindful that your purpose in life may change or evolve as you continue to learn and evolve into your true self, that is okay. As you continue to grow and evolve on this journey called life, you are bound to learn new things about yourself. You may become a brand-new person, nothing stays the same forever, not even you. Again, that is okay.

Discovering your purpose is a lifelong journey but once you figure out what your purpose is, you will notice how your life opens up to new experiences, opportunities and possibilities all around you. Just listen to your heart.

11

STOP SEEKING VALIDATION

Val·i·da·tion

/ˌvaləˈdāSH(ə)n/

NOUN

1. the action of checking or proving the validity or accuracy of something.

ARE YOU A PROCRASTINATOR? Did you know that tapping into productive self-motivation has a lot to do with how you seek validation and who you seek it from? Validation is interdependency. T is the recognition and affirmation that what you're doing is worthwhile and important. It is also the act of valuing someone else's thoughts and experiences above your own.

Validation is something that many of us are conditioned to look for (as much as 55% of people base their self value on what other people think about them). As children, we look for our parents' validation, our teachers and our friend's as well. We are conditioned to believe that we have to behave a certain way in order to make the people around us feel good.

The more we seek validation and are praised for doing things the way others want us to, the more we are conditioned to behave in a way that brings out positive responses from others. However, at some point, we're supposed to outgrow it, right? The problem is that many of us don't.

In the world of the internet and social media, just about everyone is searching for some form of validation, whether they realize it or not. With social media as prevalent as it is, more people are basing their lives around the people on their social media accounts and how they will react and respond to their posts. The fact of the matter is that we all want to feel like we belong to something or a group of people. Hence why we have so many different social media accounts that all pretty much do the same thing and have all the same friends on them.

In my opinion, there are two different types of validation—external and internal. External validation comes from the people who are around you. Ultimately, it's putting your happiness in the hands of someone outside of yourself. The thing about external validation though, it'll never be enough. You will constantly have that craving that only an outsider can fill.

I can remember back to when I was searching for a job. I would come across a position that I was interested in and instead of relying on myself, I would pick up the phone each time to get validation from others. I had to call my peers and friends and ask them if they thought I should do it. The thought was there but I always felt the need to have someone validate whether or not I could do the job. I missed out on some incredible opportunities when I did that. People will tell you that you can't do things that they won't do or that they can't do. That doesn't mean that you can't do it.

. . .

INTERNAL VALIDATION or self validation comes from you and goes hand in hand with self confidence and self esteem. It is the act of relying on your own opinion to be the driving force, proving to yourself that you are valid and accurate. Internal validation is being secure in yourself. Knowing that your feelings, opinions and decisions are perfect, regardless of the outcome. It is also the act of acceptance—accepting your thoughts, feelings and experiences and holding yourself accountable for them as well.

SELF VALIDATION IS that constant reminder of who you are and what you are capable of. It grounds you, constantly being the reminder that no one is coming to save you and making you your own savior.

LEARNING how to self validate is not an easy task. It requires that you take responsibility for your own needs. It requires that you respect and love yourself which in turn requires you to have a healthy relationship with yourself. Once you do, you will notice that you are no longer looking for people and relationships to give in order to receive.

. . .

LET me speak on self esteem really quick since I've already touched on it above. Self esteem according to Google is having confidence in one's own worth or abilities. It is also the act of liking and respecting yourself and I believe that it is a primary necessity in order to truly reach success and happiness in life.

THE MORE THAT you like yourself, then the more confidence you will have. This will result in you seeing improved performance, being more effective and being more efficient in all areas of your life. If your self esteem is low and you don't believe that you should have something or are deserving of succeeding, then you won't achieve it. That is why I believe that self esteem, self validation and success go hand in hand

FOR THOSE THAT struggle with external validation, some ways that you can stop seeking validation from outsiders is by:

TAKING A HIATUS FROM SOCIAL MEDIA. Social media is the one place that feeds our insecurities, causing us to constantly look for people that we do not interact with on a daily basis to validate us. If we don't get a sufficient amount of likes and comments on our pictures and posts, our self esteem takes a hit. Another issue social media brings to the table is the constant need to compare yourself to the social media celebrities and models. We create unrealistic expectations of how we want our lives to look based off of a snapshot of their day.

SOCIAL MEDIA HAS the power to exhaust you and lead to a burnout due to the constant stimulation and need to be validated. It's like getting your car parking validated from a store that you didn't even visit.

SPEND time getting to know yourself, loving yourself, accepting yourself and knowing that you are worthy. My belief is that a lot of us seek the approval of others because of our own insecurities. We don't believe that we are sufficient enough to make a decision on whatever we are seeking validation on. If we were secure in ourselves, we would value our own point of view and decisions. In order to build your self esteem, you have to get in touch with you.

TRUST IN YOURSELF. People will project their fears onto you if you allow them. You know what you are capable of though. Trust that you are right about yourself, because the truth is, you are right. Remember, your words and thoughts are powerful. They hold the power of life and death. Always speak life over yourself and your situation.

STOP COMPARING your progress and success to other people's success. Like flowers, we all bloom in our own appointed seasons. Our routes will differ, our journey's will differ, and our will experiences differ. Your uniqueness is what will assist you with your success. You are comparing yourself to someone who may not have had half of the experiences you've had or vice versa. Regardless, your journey is just as important as your success.

DISCOVER what it is that you need. How can you supply something that you don't know is in need? In order to be able to provide yourself with the validation that you need, you must first realize what you are in need of. What are you longing for? Look inside of yourself for the answer.

CELEBRATE YOURSELF. It doesn't matter if you perceive it as a win or a loss. Even a small win is a win, and a loss will teach you how to win… eventually. Remember, you need to validate yourself in every situation. This is a sure way to build your self esteem and confidence.

DEVELOP SOME SELF VALIDATION/SELF esteem mantras and affirmations. Repeat them daily. When you chant/repeat mantras, you release positive energy into your body. This decreases the stress, anxiety and negative thoughts that you may be having while changing your brain and your thoughts. The way that you speak to yourself is important. If it helps, you can also write your mantras and affirmations on post its and stick them around your home in places that you frequent so that you are always reminded. You can also voice record them and listen to them daily on your way to work or when you have time for yourself.

THIS CHAPTER GOES hand in hand with the next chapter… authenticity. Being in alignment with yourself will stop you from seeking the validation of outsiders. Come on, let's get into it now!

12

BE AUTHENTIC

Au·then·tic

/ô'THen(t)ik/

1. 1.

OF UNDISPUTED ORIGIN; genuine.

THERE IS a quote by Lance Secretan that goes, "Authenticity is the alignment of head, mouth, heart and feet—thinking, saying, feeling and doing the same thing—consistently. This builds trust and followers love leaders they can trust." To me, this quote describes authenticity to the T. Authenticity is being in alignment with yourself.

. . .

AUTHENTICITY IS LOST through the process of growing up and living life. As children, we are indoctrinated to fit in, adopting thoughts, beliefs and emotions that don't even belong to us. The older that we get, the more we try to balance life by finding our place in the world. Hence why we retire parts of ourselves in order to fit in, be liked or become more successful. However, how does this benefit us in the long run?

PEOPLE LOVE an authentic individual for many reasons but the main one, if you ask me, is that you always know who you are going to get. There is a certainty about people who are authentic to themselves. People who are authentic with themselves are also in line with their passions. They've taken the time to get to know themselves and understand their strengths and weaknesses,

THERE ARE people who I like to call chameleons because they will be whoever they need to be in order to get to the next level. Don't be like them. Be You. No matter the social platform I'm on or if you see me in person, I am ME. I don't know how to be anyone else.

. . .

THIS IS crucial while you are on your way to success. Once you are your authentic self, you are aware of what means the most to you. You've taken the time to get to know yourself and what matters. You cannot be swayed or pressured by the opinions of others. You trust yourself to know that your instincts are on point.

THAT DOESN'T MEAN that you cannot adapt to people and situations… you will be required to do so in order to be successful. It just means that even in adapting, you will still remain yourself. You will be able to work with those around you in a manner that is appeasing and serving to them but still serve and appease yourself. This is authenticity.

PRETENDING to be something or someone that you are not is probably the most exhausting thing in the world, yet there are so many people who do just that on a daily basis. I'm sure it isn't something they enjoy doing, they just don't trust themselves enough to be themselves. Being authentic to who you are can be scary, especially when you are going against the grain of what those around you consider to be normal. However, it becomes unbearable to be anything other than yourself after a while.

. . .

Eventually, you will start to despise yourself and those around you because you feel that you have to conform.

I've been told that my social media presence was "too loud". I backed off because of that comment being made. In a sense, that was me not being my authentic self. Allowing the opinion of outsiders to sway what I did was like me second guessing myself. Honestly, not sharing the good things on my social media platforms about my team members and friends was mentally exhausting. I'll talk about "engagement" later in the book, but this was one of my ways to celebrate the wins from my team and engage them in my business.

Some of the benefits of being authentic are:

Being able to stand firm on your decisions. You won't dread having to say no to something or someone that does not align with the vision that you have for yourself and your success. Once you have committed to your goal and taken the time to plan your goal out, you won't allow anything or anyone to distract you from your goal. Standing firm on your decisions doesn't mean that you are mean or harsh, it just means that you have your priorities aligned and you refuse to bend or break that alignment for anyone.

Having clarity about yourself and goals gives those around you clarity as well. When you are aware of what you want and don't want and what you will accept and will not accept when it comes to yourself and your goals, the people around you have no choice but to get into formation with you or move out of the way so that someone who agrees with you can. You don't have to explain yourself or the decisions that you make and the people who are around you will make those same decisions on your behalf as well.

Your ability to be authentic to yourself will aid you in determining who is genuine and who is not. People who are not for you or your success will attempt to attach themselves to you in order to aid themselves. They have the potential to hurt your success severely if you allow them to. Staying your true authentic self will remove the blinders from your eyes and give you the insight needed to see them for who they are. Trust your gut.

. . .

There will be no regrets. When you are true to yourself and your goals, there will be no room for regrets. You were aware of the decisions you had to make, you weighed your options, and you made the best decisions for your advancement. Regardless of the outcome, it was a decision that you made, rooted in the fact that you knew what was best for you.

It will let people know that they can trust in you. When you are authentic to yourself and your purpose, it will also let people (customers/clients/friends) know that you are committed and that they can trust in you to have their best interest in line as well.

Being authentic will assist you in standing out. I can't tell you how many times I've seen someone do something and before it has a chance to even live for a few minutes, it's being copied by someone else. The one good thing about being original though is that its difficult to be copied for a number of reasons. For one, you'll always be the first to do it. You will be memorable, and you will be unique. People will always remember you and your brand.

. . .

Here are some tips that you can use to help you develop authenticity:

Review the belief systems if the people around you. Many of us take family traditions and the things that we were told and taught as children to heart. However, they are some of the same things that resulted in us not being our authentic selves in this moment. By reviewing the belief systems of our family, we can begin to uncover where we got certain behaviors from and learn how to return to our authentic self.

Pinpoint the discrepancies in your life. A lot of what we say and do are done because that is what we were taught to do. With that said, what is true to you now?

Face your fears. Our fears are literally holding us back from being the people that we've always dreamt about bring and living the life in which we know belongs to us. Many of us find comfort in familiarity. The biggest fear and challenge that most of us face is dealing with unfamiliar territory. In order to stand in your authenticity, you must identify, experience, accept and let go of everything you've known. Starting with your fears,

AGAIN, being true to yourself and walking in your authenticity can be scary. It can cause you to be alone until your right tribe finds you However, to thine own self be true. The people who are meant to be in your life will find their way there soon. If they don't, that's okay too. You have to value you more than anyone or anything else. I know I do. I'm authentic from my hair to my dress. There is no other way for me to be.

13

ENGAGEMENT

En·gage·ment
/inˈgājmənt,enˈgājmənt/

NOUN

1. an arrangement to do something or go somewhere at a fixed time.

THIS CHAPTER WILL BE FUN. You can look at engagement in more ways than one. Let's get started with first one...

. . .

Someone once told me that the best place they've ever worked at, was at Best Buy during their college years. When I asked why, they told me that it was because although the store was huge, they felt seen and included. Unlike other places that they had worked at, no one behaved like they were above or better than anyone else.

Thankfully, this was a place where everyone understood their role. The employer understood how important it was in order for the people working at his company to stay engaged—they would in turn engage the customers, ensuring that they returned by forming meaningful relationships with them.

The General Manager, Supervisors, Managers, Leads and associates all got along and worked together, even outside of the job. The GM always had time for his staff, and he designated days for the employees where everyone could get together—him included.

On the days when it was nice outside, the General Manager would buy everyone food or host a huge cook out in the back of the Best Buy building so that all of the staff could spend time together eating and hanging out. He treated everyone with the same respect, and he made it clear that everyone was necessary for the success of the business.

He understood that happy and engaged employees made for happy and engaged customers… customers who would return and in turn make the store successful.

Due to the General Managers understanding that happy and engaged employees made for happy and engaged customers he in turn had customers who would return and make his store successful as well. The people who worked there worked hard at their job, staying up to date on new products, crossing over into other departments to assist customers with purchases on items that they weren't required to know about.

This also goes to show that when people feel engaged, they are more likely to go above and beyond to succeed and see the company succeed as well. Engagement also leads to long term employee retention. People are less likely to leave their jobs when they feel engaged.

I believe that as the CEO (Chief Engagement Officer) of any business or organization, one of the most important things you can do is to engage your staff as well as your customers. You have to be engaged with the people and you have to make work fun. Your employees or associates are people, not robots. They are human beings with feelings. When employees are engaged, they give more of themselves resulting in a high quality of work.

To drive engagement, I feel that you must celebrate even the small wins because eventually, they become big wins. When you are engaged, you understand the culture and what makes your team happy and what they take pride in. That's how you celebrate.

Another form of engagement is through social media. Social media provides individuals and brands the opportunity to get recognized and create a following. This is how a lot of people seek connections with brands and people. Social media engagement has a major impact on businesses, especially now in the midst of the pandemic. It affects everything from customer loyalty to brand awareness.

Social media permits you to build relationships and learn from the community and customers that we serve in regard to how we can improve their experiences not just with us but overall. This allows us to build a better product for people to use by knowing exactly what they want.

Social media engagement measures the way that people are interacting with your social media accounts and content. It can include likes and favorites, comments, DMs, replies, shares, stories and retweets, reels, saves, clicks and mentions. Engagement is a great way to measure whether the content you're creating is actually resonating with your audience.

I can remember working in an environment where what they enjoyed was music and dancing. TikTok was trending and they wanted to celebrate a win by doing a TikTok. I was so fearful because I can’t dance! However, I made it work. The current trend at that time was “Something New”. Instead of joining the actual dance, I jumped out of a box at the end. It worked! Between several social channels, they had more than 50,000 views and the world could see their accomplishments! Engagement matters.

. . .

Some ways that you can boost or maintain your social media engagement is by:

Be social. Just being on social media is not enough. You must interact with the people on social media as well. This means leaving comments and responding to your comments and mentions as well.

Get to know the unique algorithm of each social media account you use. Familiarizing yourself with the algorithms presents you with the ability to boost your engagement. Things like when is the best time for you to post, who sees and interacts with your posts the most, and what hashtags get the best response are all important algorithms that dictate how people see your post and interact with them.

Maintain a consistent and authentic social media voice. Humanizing your brand is important. It's what encourages people to give feedback freely and talk about your brand in a positive light. Establishing a brand voice is extremely important if multiple people manage your social media accounts.

. . .

Know your audience. If you don't know who you are talking to, how can you engage them? Language, tone and resources vary based on who you are speaking to. In order for your messages to resonate, you need to know who your target is.

Keep your response times quick. Remember what I said a few chapters ago about instant gratification? Yeah, well, that applies here too. People want to feel like they have you at the tip of their fingertips if they need you. For that reason alone, having a speedy response time can lead to increased customer satisfaction.

Schedule your post. I can't tell you how many times I've had a busy day and that resulted in me forgetting to post. There were also many times when I knew that I needed to post but I just didn't know what to post. Now, there are sites and apps that will allow you to schedule your post and post it for you at the time and date that you specify. How dope is that?

Make sure that your feed flows. Profiles with consistent colors and themes flow better and look more attractive. Develop a color scheme and a pattern to help your media pages stand out.

ON THE FLIP SIDE, in order to succeed, you must engage yourself in your goal. You cannot just write it down or speak it out loud and expect it to happen on its own. Again, we're back at planning. If you don't engage your plan and execute it, you might as well call it a day. In order to see real success, you have to put in the work.

14

SUMMARY

If you've made it through this book, then you know that there are many important factors of success. Each factor that we have discussed throughout this manual has been just as important as the next. Together, we've gone over twelve of the traits that I believe are extremely important for success. However, again, please note that those are not the only factors that determine success. I just believe that they are the most important factors.

Again, based on my own understanding of success and what I equate it to, there are about 12 steps, give or take, that I feel like need to be completed and followed in order to reach the full level of success. Those steps included planning, spending time alone, experiencing failure, staying well rested, being self accountable, staying unbiased and listening. Staying away from comfortably (complacency), having a good mentor and patience, staying true to your purpose, not seeking validation, staying authentic and maintaining engagement.

To further assist you with retaining the information provided in this book, I'm going to give the definitions once again of each of the 12 steps as well as a short description.

1. Planning is a detailed proposal for doing or achieving something. Planning is simply how you intend to achieve your goal. Without planning, you are bound to fail every time.
2. Alone (spending time alone) is simply put, the art of being alone. Having time alone gives you time to focus on you without the distractions of family and friends around you. It gives you the time to come to terms with the things that you truly desire opposed to the things that those around you want for you.
3. Failure is the lack of success. Ultimately, it's about perception. If you perceive your experience as a bad thing then that is what it is. However, you stand to learn about yourself and your task through failure… if you pay attention.
4. Rest is ceasing work or movement in order

to relax, refresh, and or recover strength. Rest is very important. It's kind of like a shower for your mind, cleaning the previous day off of yourself, saving you from burnout and allowing you to connect back to you.

5. Self accountability is the act or condition of being held accountable or responsible for self. A mindset that promotes growth through ownership of your failures and successes.
6. Listening is the act of giving one their undivided attention. This is an important trait because every idea comes from listening and every relationship that you have must entail listening. It's how you build interpersonal relationships. Therefore, you should always take the time to actively listen.
7. Complacency is the act of getting comfortable and feeling of smug or uncritical satisfaction with oneself or one's achievements. In order to avoid becoming complacent, you should always reevaluate and reflect on your success and yourself. Your only competition is you.
8. Mentorship is the relationship that is formed through guidance provided by a mentor, especially an experienced person in a company or educational institution to a mentee. Mentorships are beneficial. They

promote self confidence, self awareness, promotions, and increased knowledge and engagement.

9. Patience is the capacity to accept or tolerate delay, trouble, or suffering without getting angry or upset. Having the internet at the tip of our fingers has spoiled us, causing us to lose the trait of patience. However, patience is needed in order to see your aspirations and goals through.
10. Purpose is the reason for which something is done or created or for which something exists. Knowing your purpose gives your life meaning while keeping you centered, focused and in tune with what really matters to you and what you want out of your life.
11. Validation is the action of checking or proving the validity or accuracy of something. The only form of validation that you should ever want or take into consideration is self validation. Self validation is the constant reminder that you are enough. It's knowing that you are capable if saving yourself because you have the responsibility and have the confidence to make the best decisions for you.
12. Lastly, engagement is an arrangement to do something or go somewhere at a fixed time.

> Engaging your staff in turn leads to engaged clientele. When people feel like they are a part of something, they give more of themselves in order to see it grow.

Over the years, I have tackled each of these twelve tasks at some point throughout my journey to success, more than once. Now that I am climbing the ladder to success again, I am once again enthralled in them. I am consistently and repeatedly planning while creating specific and actionable goals that are motivating and fulfilling. I'm ensuring that all of my goals have a date listed on them as to when I would like to achieve them so that I can ensure that it aligns with my life's purpose, as well.

I am ensuring that I get as much rest as I need so that I am refreshed and operating with a clear mind. I am holding myself accountable for my actions or lack thereof when I am slacking. I'm also listening to those who have traveled a similar road to success as the one that I am currently traveling on to ensure that I don't make an avoidable mistake.

I will not spend time looking for other people outside of myself to validate me or my success. My life is only going to be lived out by me. No one else has to deal with the consequences of any of my actions or decisions. Despite everyone clouding me and my decision to be different, there are still people who will think that they know what is best for me and my life, I will not listen to them. I will be patient with myself and my success.

Remaining in my purpose is important to me as well. I want to remain authentic to myself and my purpose. I know that if I stray, the outcome may not be a favorable one for me. Lastly, I want to stay engaged in every way imaginable.

There may be some steps to success that you may feel that I am missing… for instance, like writing down your goals (which we did speak about it briefly in a previous chapter). Have you ever tried writing it down somewhere? If it's written, it shall be.

If you believe that there are steps that are missing that you may benefit from on your path to success, be sure to add them. Again, success is subjective. The steps you take to reach success don't necessarily have to be the same steps that I take to reach success. Do what works for you, just make sure that you get it done. That is the most important part of this all.

If there is anything that you have gotten from this book, I hope it's that at the end of the day, success… *your* success, lies in *your* hands and is determined by you and you only. Even with me giving you all of these steps and traits that I think are needed to achieve success, if you don't consistently put in the work and show up for yourself, you'll always be where you are right at this moment.

Not to say that there is anything wrong with that., maybe where you are is enough for you… remember, success is subjective. So, yeah… maybe the success you have right now is fulfilling to you, that's fine. I can't say the same though. For me, this is just a starting point. My true point of success is many moons away.

LET'S CHAT!

Want to stay connected?! Find me on social media.

facebook.com/natoya.holden

linkedin.com/in/natoya-champion-a0b086158